FAITHFUL HOUND

BEDDGELERT
AND THE TRUTH ABOUT ITS LEGEND

The original boulder and two slate tablets, telling the tale in English and Welsh, form the basis of the grave today.

Faithful Hound

Beddgelert
and the truth about its legend

Michael Senior

First published in 2009

© Michael Senior/Llygad Gwalch

© Llygad Gwalch 2009

ISBN: 978-1-84524-150-6

Cover design: Sian Parri

Published by Llygad Gwalch,
12 Iard yr Orsaf, Llanrwst, Wales LL26 0EH
tel: 01492 624031
fax: 01492 641502
email: books@carreg-gwalch.com
website: www.carreg-gwalch.com

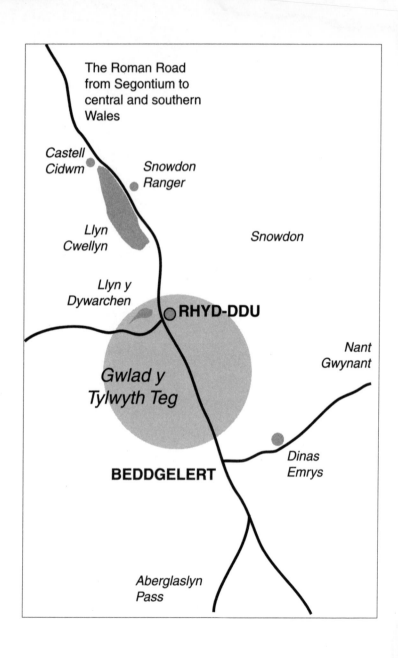

Contents

A bronze statue of a hound ties the legend to the name 'Bryn y Bedd', site of the ruins of an old cowshed.

The tomb, or what is said to be the tomb, of Gelert, stands in a beautiful meadow just below the precipitous side of Cerrig Llan ... Who is there acquainted with the legend, whether he believes that the dog lies beneath those stones or not, can visit them without exclaiming with a sigh, 'Poor Gelert!'

George Borrow, *Wild Wales*

WILD WALES
ITS PEOPLE, LANGUAGE
AND SCENERY

BY GEORGE BORROW

" Their Lord they shall praise,
Their language they shall keep,
Their land they shall lose,
Except Wild Wales.'
TALIESIN : *Destiny of the Britons*

LONDON
JOHN MURRAY, ALBEMARLE STREET, W.
1923

ONE

EVER FAITHFUL

'Situated at the junction of three vales, and closely surrounded by mountains': the phrasing in the guidebook of 1891 can scarcely be improved on, and modern descriptions only seek to add their honest and simple praise. All are agreed that it is 'undoubtedly Snowdonia's loveliest village', or 'without doubt one of the most attractive villages in the whole of the United Kingdom.' Coming into the heart of it today one is simply amazed by the miracle that no administrative vandals have succeeded in obliterating this

George Borrow walking in Snowdonia

George Borrow's portrait and signature in the Goat, Beddgelert, today

vulnerable charm. Yet it and its surroundings remain unscathed, as they were when George Borrow visited in 1854: 'Truly, the valley of Gelert is a wondrous valley, rivalling for grandeur and beauty any vale either in the Alps or Pyrenees.' It is so unexpectedly perfect, in fact, that it obliges you to exaggerate.

With so much natural beauty, so much integrity and such a depth of historic significance, what need has Beddgelert of an addition which is, to say the least, superimposed: its famous 'grave'? Yet even the most serious modern literature has to admit that this is its best-known feature. The official website has it as an appendix, and simply reports the story as inscribed on the stone at the site. You know it already, because everybody does. It hardly needs a stone plaque or the authority of the web to tell us. Returning from hunting, Llywelyn thinks his dog has killed his child. He kills the dog.

It was all a terrible mistake, and is reflected in a Welsh proverb, *mor ffôl â'r gŵr a laddes ei filgi*, 'as foolish as the man who slew his greyhound'. The connection of the story to the place relies on the addition that in contrition the prince sited a grave and monument there for the dog. The undoubted fact that *Bedd* means 'grave', and that this is perhaps unique in Welsh place-names, gives at least the need to explain this rare occurrence, which we shall in due course be dealing with in this book. The story in its final form is, as the National Museums' *Welsh Folk Tales* points out, onomastic. It sets out to explain a name. We shall see that this was not originally its purpose.

The grave itself is out to the side of the village, and in such a spot as one may appreciate the siting of the settlement of Beddgelert on a rare flat green plain. One can see from there the church and the roofs of one or two other buildings where they squat around their nexus at the bridging point of the rivers, that link of communications which gives the village its focus – so that you can appreciate its geography better from here than when actually in its streets. The Royal Goat Hotel proclaims its slightly separate significance, larger than any other building and overlooking the village's layout. The grave itself is formal and municipal, with

The 'grave' is now in the care of the National Trust

11

Hafod y Llan – another National Trust property near Beddgelert

its railings and its approach by concrete footpath, winding along the riverbank and across the field. Only something about its great lump of stone proclaims an ancient Welshness which just succeeds in defying cynicism.

At almost any time of the year there may be one or two people there. A sporadic trickle in the winter, it turns in season into a steady flow. They may come from any part of the world. The sight itself is a tribute to Gelert's perennial staying power.

'Gelert's Grave' is on land owned by the National Trust, along with an area of 963 acres in the surroundings of Beddgelert, upland farms extending as far as the top of Snowdon in the form of much mountain land and natural woodland, properties including Hafod Garegog to the south of the parish, Aberglaslyn Pass itself, Craflwyn, on the way into Nant Gwynant, and Hafod y Porth and Hafod y Llan on Snowdon. The Trust began to buy property here in the 1930's, when Aberglaslyn Pass was purchased and Hafod Lwyfog on the southern slopes of Nant Gwynant, and the bulk of the ownership followed from the 1998 campaign to 'Save Snowdon', which arose from the decision of the owner of this side of the mountain to sell. The result is that now the Trust is the largest employer in the village (though this amounts to some twenty people), and is actively engaged in farming and of course in conservation of its woodland. It faces the formidable task of trying to reverse the exuberant spread of common rhododendrons, seeded from ornamental varieties in gardens, which now clog the surrounding hillsides and have seriously affected the area's ecology. Although pretty when in flower, these *rhododendron ponticum* blanket the ground and obliterate the wide variety of native flora. Their ability to grow on steep terrain, out of reach of machinery,

The 'grave' near Afon Glaslyn in Beddgelert,
with the ruins of the old cowshed in the distance

13

Looking from behind Gelert's stone back towards the village

Another view of the hound's statue within the massive stone walls
of the old cowshed

means that much of the work of eradicating them has to be done by hand by suitably agile people.

Down here in the village the ownership also includes the old cowshed near the grave, in which is a bronze statue of a dog, a work commissioned by a community project formed in 2000. Neither the work of art nor the cowshed make any claim that this was actually the spot famous for the tragic error, though the fine stone slabs of the ancient building contribute an added atmosphere of ancient land use to what would otherwise be a naturally scenic spot.

TWO

TRAVELLERS' TALES

Although its special position in people's imaginations had started early, Beddgelert seriously began to take up its prominence among Wales's favoured places during the 18th century. We shall trace in a later chapter the specific rise in its popularity which is so closely connected with the story about the dog, but that itself could perhaps not have arisen if the village had not already achieved a favoured role in the Romantic movement, possessing as it did so many of the distinguishing qualities of the 'picturesque' ideal: isolation, a certain mysterious foreignness, wild mountainous surroundings, tranquil river banks and meadows.

Several of the background factors of history coincide here, converging forces carving out the landscape in which events take place: the forces of international politics, for instance, of national economics, of European culture and of social convention. In several relevant senses the eighteenth century was the 'Age of Revolutions', in which radical and far-reaching changes took place for quite separate reasons, and what we see happening so unexpectedly in the wildness of Wales is the result of the convergence of several of these.

A pan-European improvement in transport – better roads enabling the use of faster and more comfortable carriages – had combined with increased personal wealth and consequent greater leisure to give rise to a new habit of travelling, as part of an educational expansion which saw wider knowledge in general as of value in itself. The Industrial Revolution was a part of this, releasing new wealth into the old landowning classes, encouraging trade between countries to take a faster and more reliable form, promoting a love of the things which were already by then perceived to be vulnerable to destruction. As Britain became a land of dark satanic mills people went to wonder at the Alps, and as our medieval cities became squeezed in the grip of workers' terraces they came to appreciate the glory that was Rome. The idea of the Grand Tour was far from new, but it had mainly been a part of the education of the elite; now all of an artistic inclination could take their sketch books to the Rhine and the Aegean.

Another revolution changed all of that. People continued to go to France in the immediate aftermath of the fall of the Bastille, but the situation became increasingly uncomfortable and with the start of the 'Reign of Terror' in 1793 the French internal upheaval became an international affair, and Britain and France became officially at war. This culminated in 1803 with the start of the confrontation with Napoleon which was to put France and consequently the whole of continental Europe out of bounds to us for a further dozen years.

It was then discovered that we had our own version of the Alps, and in place of classical temples and theatres we had our Gothic ruins, chiefly in the form of gaunt and evocative medieval castles and the suggestive shells of the long-dissolved monasteries. A whole world of what had by then become the distant British past was rediscovered, and with it the temporarily lost literature of a previous Britain – Arthur, Merlin, the Lady of the Lake.

Thomas Pennant was something of a pioneer in the new discovery of an old Britain, since he published his first volume of *Tours in Wales* in 1778, writing about journeys he had made in 1773

Thomas Pennant

and 1776. But Pennant was unusual too among our travellers through having been born in the place he was writing about, a Flintshire man educated at Wrexham. He had in any case travelled widely on the continent while it was still possible, and he wrote about northern Wales with the same sense of investigating a foreign country, which, still then without through roads or regular traffic, it must to most people have appeared. Pennant was sympathetic to its ancient authenticity, being Welsh himself, but he was visiting late enough to see the onset of anachronism in its contrasting character. He rode down from the Snowdon range through Nant Gwynant, and after a 'pleasant, but short ride' he came to the place of the junction of three vales at Beddgelert: 'Its situation is the fittest in the world to inspire religious meditation …' He describes the church in some detail, and his information on the monastic history of the settlement will concern us again. He does not mention any other building, and there seems to have been no formal accommodation since he came back after some excursions to Drws y Coed and Nantlle and in Beddgelert 'made a coarse lodging'.

Pennant's work was edited for the new 1810 publication by John Rhys, described by the publisher as 'Professor of Celtic in the University of Oxford', who added some notes 'chiefly indicative of the changes which have occurred during that period', the thirtysomething years since its first publication. Here there occurs one of significance, since by 18l0 Beddgelert was on its way to future fame:

> The traveller will now find a small, but very comfortable inn at Bedd Kelert. The improvement of the houses of accommodation throughout *North Wales* has of late years been very considerable. Ed.

John Rhys

As it happens we have conformation of this change from another literary traveller, the Rev. Bingley. It is significant that these writers considered it important enough to mention the state of accommodation in Beddgelert, but we must suppose that both Caernarfon and Capel Curig were too far away from the south side of Snowdon for one to be able to visit that area in a day and get home to lodging. Part of the problem was the state of the roads, and part the special characteristic of the area which explains their presence in the first place: there was a lot to do there, a lot to see, including the need to climb Snowdon.

The Rev. W. Bingley came first (from Cambridge, via Caernarfon) in 1798 and again in 1801, and he found the inn ('or rather public house') on both occasions to be 'one of the worst and most uncomfortable houses' he had ever had to stay at. He gives us, characteristically, a lively and graphic description. The first time, he had had to stay for three nights in a room in which the floor, ceiling and partition were 'so full of large holes, as to seem only an apology for separation from the rest of the house.' It was dirty and infested by fleas. By the second time he came things had improved, though if at that establishment evidently through the threat of impending competition. It seems from his account that in 1801 the house being built by Mr. Jones of Bryntirion 'on the other side of the river, at a few hundred yards distance' was not yet open, but by the time he writes it 'now affords excellent accommodations', and his appended directory in the published version of 1814 states: 'At Beddgelert there is a very comfortable inn called the Beddgelert Hotel.' It seems clear that the place where Bingley stayed was what is now the Saracen's Head, originally a farm which became called Tŷ Ucha' during the eighteenth century.

Bingley's three nights at Beddgelert are explained by the programme he packed in. He stopped on the way up from

The Saracen's Head inn,
originally a farmhouse known as Tŷ Uchaf

Caernarfon to climb Moel Eilio, above Llyn Cwellyn. He notes that the road, coming this way, 'is in general very excellent; being the great road from Caernarvonshire into South Wales'. The way the Romans came, in other words, the link, that is, between Segontium and Maridunum, now Carmarthen, by way of the junction post up at Trawsfynydd where it was joined by the route from Canovium and Chester.

The road shows no sign now of being Roman, and its curves and winding line along the contours must have caused the legions some distaste, as must the wriggling fall to the head of Traeth Mawr and the subsequent rise past Maen Twrog. It is essentially an old Welsh coach route now, such as took the mail in the early days of turnpikes, bounded by traditional walls and served by robust bridges.

Inland it was a different world, and the bulk of Snowdon stood in the way. There was 'a horse-path through this vale [Nant Gwynant] to Capel Curig, and Llanrwst.' Here perhaps is part of the explanation for the focus of attention on Beddgelert: it was not as isolated and remote when viewed from Caernarfon as from the other half of the county, beyond the mountains. The road then carries him past Llyn Cwellyn, at the end of which he notes, but does not visit, a rocky outcrop known as Castell Cidwm. This, through local lore, gives a distinct and strange link to a memory of the Roman passage through this valley.

It was the home and lookout of a giant, called Cidwm. Nothing more about him is known, Bingley says, except the occurrences of one momentous day. The emperor Constantine was marching his army up the valley, himself taking up the rear while his mother, the empress Helen, led the train about ten miles ahead. The giant Cidwm picked out the emperor and fired an arrow which killed him. News was taken through the ranks to his mother, and he was buried

The crags of Castell Cidwm rise above the road from Caernarfon as it approaches Llyn Cwellyn

there, 'in the meadow at the lower end of the lake, in a place now called Bedd y mab'. Bingley says this is one of 'those traditional legends, that defy all attempts at investigation'. Yet it can be stated that Castell Cidwm, though blackly rearing from the road, and undoubtedly offering an irresistible lookout over the route up through the valley, is a natural feature, not the fortification of a giant; that Bedd y mab is a site which can no longer be identified; and that the emperor Constantine (who did visit Britain, but not, as far as is known, Wales) died at Nicomedia, a town to the east of the Sea of Marmara, now Izmit in Turkey, preparing for a campaign into Persia, in 337, and was buried (of course) in Constantinople. Nor is it entirely true that the tale defies all attempts at investigation, since Bingley seems to have stumbled on something of authentic local interest. Cidwm does not occur elsewhere in folktale, as an emperor-killer or as a giant, though the name of his

Llyn Cwellyn

rock in mentioned in George Borrow's account, where it is concluded that though Cidwm means wolf, and so the outcrop of rock Wolf's Castle, it could have been the refuge of a robber-chieftain, since 'cidwm in the old Welsh is frequently applied to a ferocious man'. In other words, it is clear that neither Borrow nor his informants have heard of the giant. The story's specification of Constantine as the general leading the army arises from a confusion of empresses, since there were two Helen's, the one being the mother of Constantine, wife of Constantius, whereas quite another Helen, or Elen, daughter of a British chief called Eudaf, was the wife and empress of Magnus Maximus, who is associated in the story with Segontium, as Macsen Wledig.

Bingley broke his journey to visit Llyn y Dywarchen, 'the lake of the turf', an unremarkable pool which had been given unexpected fame by Giraldus Cambrensis, inserted in his account of his journey

Llyn y Dywarchen

among some references to this area which seem to be afterthoughts. When Gerald came in the 12th century it had, he tells us, a floating island in it which the wind drove from one side to the other, carrying cattle feeding on it, – and indeed Pennant tells us that in the 18th this was still there, about nine yards long. The lake lay in a 'turbery', an area of peat cutting, and the 'island' was a detached piece of the bank held together by matted roots. It was still there too at the turn of that century when Bingley came, with a small willow tree on it. The lake now is used for fishing, but is otherwise remote and unremarkable in its moorland setting. There is indeed an island in it, but it is definitely not moving. It sits like a lost whale, rocked-walled, a small pine tree on its top.

Bingley later tells of his outings into the Aberglaslyn Pass and up to Nant Gwynant and Dinas Emrys, all of which form part of the build-up of romantic interest in the area which motivated the

Snowdon Ranger

'picturesque' travellers of the next few decades. In his narrative, however, having arrived at Beddgelert, he now launches into the story of the dog, the subject of our next few chapters.

Another notable traveller here at this time was George Borrow, who came towards harvest time in the year 1854. Like Bingley he came up from Caernarfon, a walk of thirteen miles which he didn't start until three in the afternoon, finally arriving in Beddgelert at night. On the way he meets none other than the Snowdon Ranger himself, whose house on the shore of Llyn Cwellyn is still known by the title which he appears to have given himself. 'A ranger means a guide, sir' his son-in-law explains, 'and he has named the house after him the Snowdon Ranger'. The house is still so called, though expanded now to form a popular Youth Hostel.

Borrow notes that Mynydd Mawr (which he wrongly identifies as Mynydd Drws y Coed) seen from the Betws valley looks 'just like a couchant elephant', a description which fits it rather impressively, its huge bulk declining to a crumpled trunk nuzzling into the valley. He stops at a mill below Llyn Cwellyn, where he asks about the ownership of the land. Mr. Williams, he is told, by the mill lady, possesses some part of Moel Eilio.

'And who is Mr. Williams?' I said.

'Who is Mr. Williams?' said the miller's wife. 'Ho, ho! What a stranger you must be to ask me who is Mr. Williams.'

The Snowdon Ranger is richly scathing about the new popularity of 'Bethgelert' – 'that trumpery place'. Those who go there to ascend Snowdon are fools: 'The place to ascend Snowdon from is my house.' From that you can also have the best guide in Wales. '... whereas the guides of Beth Gelert – but I say nothing.' When Borrow finally gets to his accommodation in the village we hear much more about his fellow travellers, who are caricatured ruthlessly, but nothing, disappointingly, about the inn itself. It was evidently not remarkable enough by then to draw comments such as those made by Bingley. Borrow then has a chapter about the story of the dog, tragically killed 'from an unlucky apprehension', in telling which he introduces some details which are at variance with Bingley's and so will interest us later.

A view of Beddgelert from the inside during that century shows us what Borrow and Bingley approached so enthusiastically from a distance: a self-confident little community, secure in its awareness of its own basis in history. It is thanks to the Rev. D. E. Jenkins that we have a detailed record of the village then, and an account of how it came about.

David Erwyd Jenkins was actually from Carmarthenshire, but found himself posted as a Calvinistic Methodist minister to Porthmadog in the 1890's. There he came across a series of articles by William Jones (bon at Beddgelert in 1829) published in the

Welsh-language periodical *Y Brython* in 1861. These originated in an essay entitled 'The Antiquities and Folk-Lore of Bedd Gelert' which had been submitted to the Eisteddfod held at Beddgelert in 1860 and there shared the prize. Jones won (on the subject of Conwy) again at the National Eisteddfod in Conwy in 1861. Subsequently he specialized in geology, and established a reputation as an antiquarian. His background qualified him particularly to deal with Beddgelert, since his family came from there and he himself was born there.

Jenkins's book *(Bedd Gelert, Its Facts, Fairies and Folklore)*, published in 1899, is a translation and re-ordering of Jones's articles, and an opportunity in some cases to update them. In considering publication he wrote to John Rhys, Professor of Celtic Studies at Jesus College, Oxford, Pennant's editor and the author (by then) of an article on Welsh Fairy Tales in the *Cymmrodorion* and shortly afterwards of the magisterial *Celtic Folklore*. Although Rhys had not met either author he knew of Jones's work, and supplied an introduction to Jenkins's book, which consequently comes with the weight of that authority.

Jenkins's book starts, as no doubt Jones's articles do, with factual, dutiful notes about the parish. It is only gradually as his subject expands from Beddgelert into other worlds that his imagination is equivalently released, and his own enthusiastically academic approach to folklore and literature become apparent. He recognizes the limits to Beddgelert's history, since the references to its ecclesiastical origins are slight, and the village has grown from an agricultural context independent of its roots in a Priory. Mineral working in the area was sporadic and after a period of activity in the 19th century it petered out. The Sygun mine, on the Nant Gwynant approach to the village, is the present representative of this period. It closed to production in 1903, but reopened as a

The Sygun mine, now a tourist facility, was one of Beddgelert's attempts to exploit its copper

tourist attraction in 1986. It now offers a self-guided underground tour and some outdoor walks.

The copper of the parish, Jenkins says, 'has far too many impurities ever to pay for its working'. The bed of Nant Colwyn is composed of slate, but he (and we) may be relieved that it has not proved worth exploiting. He ventures an expression of personal bias here: '… we cannot say that we wish to see these magnificent old mountains torn and scarred by mines and quarries'. Jenkins rightly points thus to the element of chance which has left Beddgelert rural, in contrast to the industrialized mountain towns of Bethesda and Llanberis. Of the village which developed in this mainly agricultural world, he tells us that the Calvinistic Methodist Chapel was first built in 1794, and enlarged between 1826 and 59; the second, Congregational Chapel having come along in 1852.

Jenkins is conscious of the part played in the rise of Beddgelert by its hostelries, a recognition that outside influences have always been a factor in its makeup. To begin with its accommodation and catering seems to have been divided in a simple alternative, between Tŷ Uchaf, later the Saracen's Head, and Tŷ Isaf, now known as Llywelyn's Cottage. The latter was a pub in the late 17th century, from which time the present building (now in the ownership of the National Trust) dates.

Tŷ Uchaf, which became the Saracen's Head in the late 19th century, was originally a farm, and is the lodging house mentioned above in which Bingley was obliged to stay. In keeping with the tight-knit structure of the village the daughter of its first recorded landlord (Captain Roberts) married the second son of David Prichard, first landlord of the Goat, and they took the Saracen's Head over on his death. When Bingley remarks that facilities for

Bwthyn Llywelyn, originally an inn known as Tŷ Isaf

The Royal Goat was originally 'The Bedd Gelert Hotel', and came to be called Royal after the visit by Prince Arthur in the 1870's

visitors were being built 'on the other side of the river' he records the historic importance of building what became the Goat Hotel.

The other side of the river from the Saracen's Head, being the west banks of the Colwyn and the Glaslyn, was part of an estate owned by the family of Hengwrt, the daughter of which had married a certain Thomas Jones, of Bryntirion, near Bangor. Mr. Jones was, according to Jenkins, 'a gentleman of liberal and patriotic spirit, more anxious to serve his generation than himself' and 'he looked upon his acquired estate as a trust which had been handed over to him for the purpose of improvement.' Inheriting the undeveloped part of the parish through his wife he took an interest in Beddgelert's main defect, its lack of decent accommodation, and 'determined to wipe away its reproach by building a new inn'.

It was called the Bedd Gelert Hotel. The sign over the door was a reference to the crest of the coat of arms of the Bryntirion family: a goat climbing among mountains, with the motto *Patria mea petra*, 'my country is a rock'. From that it naturally came to be called the Goat, and the quality Royal got added after a visit by Prince Arthur in the 1870's.

Thomas Jones, for all his public spirit, was not personally inclined to run the business. He wanted it to be the best of its kind, and by luck came upon the man who turned out to be more than capable of fulfilling the role of tenant-manager. David Prichard, a man from South Wales who had arrived in the area of few years earlier, married a girl from Bwlch Mwrchan whom he met while she was in service at Craig y Don in Anglesey. The young couple then with one child came to run the Bedd Gelert Hotel as soon as it was built, in 1802.

ENTREPREN

Jenkins says Prichard came to the Beddgele\
northern Wales) because he was already in \
had met his wife-to-be elsewhere and followe\
that we do not know anything about him until h\
to the Goat. Jenkins speaks highly of them bot\
way they ran the pub and their popularity in the v___, which 'the
respect with which they are spoken of to this day amply proves'.

Naturally Jenkins praises too 'The skill with which he used the
Gelert legend for the purpose of increasing his own business and for
making popular his adopted little village', a more generous
response than by some to what is often regarded as a form of fraud.
The exact means by which he brought this about is recounted in the
words of Jenkins's sources, the articles by Jones in *Y Brython*,
written in 1859 and published in 1861, which he translates as
follows:

The legend is universal and timeless, and it does not
traditionally belong to Beddgelert, but was

> brought to the parish by the late David Prichard, the Goat
> Hotel, who was a native of South Wales. It was he, along with
> William Prichard, the parish clerk, and Richard Edwards, of
> Pen y Bont Fach, who raised the stone that is exhibited today
> on the spot that was afterwards called 'the Dog's Grave.' We
> heard the latter two saying that they tried to raise up a large

David Pritchard and his helpers marked 'Gelert's Grave' with a massive boulder

stone which lay on the northern side of the hillock, but that
they failed; and they carried the present stone from another
place in order to put it where it now is.

This is as near as we are ever going to get to an eye-witness
report, and we have no reason to doubt it. Its incidental detail
makes it credible. It does not explain, of course, the immense and
immediate success of the fictional story. The fact that it thrived so
positively is due partly to its own strengths as a story, of course, but
a large part of its blossoming was due to the sort of place which
Beddgelert is: a valley rich in the fostering of imagination, in which
anything can be believed. It is clear that the sort of people it has
always attracted are drawn to it because of its otherworldly air.

Prichard and his accomplices chose the spot because it was on
land which went with the hotel. Indeed he farmed this area seriously
himself, appearing to know something of farming already. He

cleared the stones from the fields and drained the marshy areas, 'so that' (Jenkins's informant tells us) 'in a few years he had made his poor holding an excellent farm, and he received a silver cup as an acknowledgement of his industry from the owners of the surrounding land.' This enterprise, and the enlargement of the hotel, made him 'very well off'. But then he was, we are told, 'very fond of money'.

The motive for the grave-construction is clear though not originally made explicit: David Prichard was in the process of promoting the popularity of his new business. But Jones (and hence Jenkins) goes one step further. He says that Prichard did not just build the grave, but imported into Beddgelert the whole story, 'which does not traditionally belong to the parish'. 'It had no place at all in the folk-lore of this part until it was brought to the parish by the late David Prichard, the Goat Hotel, who was a native of South Wales.'

We are not told in this only authentic version whether the dog's grave was arbitrarily placed, or had some prior significance. It has often been assumed that because it is itself a slight mound, and has some apparently ancient stones on it, it was in fact already a grave, and the explanation of the name of the town. After all, since place-names on the whole do not mislead, we may feel sure there is a grave here somewhere. Yet it seems agreed that the mound on which Prichard and colleagues placed the dog's memorial stone is natural, a probably glacial deposit.

Jenkins himself, in his extensive evidence, accidentally provides room for doubt on this. He cites a passage from Joseph Jacobs's *Celtic Fairy Tales* which in turn quotes another Jones, an Edward Jones who published a book called *Musical (and Poetical) Relics of the Welsh Bards*, in 1784. There Jones reproduces an *englyn* about a skilful *(celfydd)* dog called Cilhart of the cantref of Eifionydd, famed for stag hunting. The significance here is that in his second edition of 1794 he adds a footnote which tells the Gelert story: a wolf entered the house of Prince Llywelyn and when he came home he found his dog, Kill-hart, covered in blood and the child's cradle overturned. He drew the wrong conclusion and his sword. Here then is the first mention we are aware of, of the name of the dog which became Gelert, of the wolf, the child, Llywelyn's connection and the unfortunate mistake.

Jacobs assumes that Spencer got his theme for the poem which then promoted the story, which he first published privately in 1800, from this note of Jones's. Jenkins says not. 'No, we are sure it was not. It was David Prichard, the first landlord of the Royal Goat Hotel, who came into the parish about the year 1793, and hailed from South Wales.' He was, Jenkins says, a great story–teller, and soon became a centre of attraction. The story 'was well known in South Wales'. Edward Jones, preparing the second edition of his *Relics* heard it from him, and added the note. 'In 1784, when he was bringing out his first edition, Mr. Prichard was not there; but he was there in good time for the second.'

There are a number of things wrong with this. First, Jenkins seems to know the date by which Prichard came to Beddgelert, and clearly something must have occurred to enlighten Jones between 1784 and 1794; but the supposition that Prichard was a skilled raconteur is surely pure speculation on Jenkins's part, based perhaps on the story of his construction of the grave. And there is equally no reason to suppose that he brought the story from South Wales, where it 'was well known'. It might have been, of course, because it was well-known everywhere, as we shall see – but just as likely in Beddgelert. Why would it have been David Prichard who told Jones the story? The later interpretation has him wishing to promote the fame of the village for the sake of his business at the

Goat. But he was not landlord of the Goat then, because it was not built. It started to be constructed in 1801 and was open in 1802.

Similarly when Spencer wrote and published his poem (first by a private printing on 11th August 1800 at Dolmelynllyn, Madocks's house at Dolgellau) there is no independent suggestion that he had met Prichard. We do however have firm testimony that he was influenced by Bingley: 'The following beautiful stanzas, which the author, the honourable W.R. Spencer, has so obligingly allowed me to insert here, are founded on the above tradition. They were written at Dolmelynllyn, the seat of W. A. Madocks, Esq. after a perusal of the story as related in my *Tour round North Wales*.'

The *Tour round North Wales* was the earlier version of Bingley's *North Wales*, published in 1800 and based on his journey of 1798 – and so capable of being influenced by the same source of information as Jones was, in his second edition of the *Relics* in 1794. Bingley too connects the dog of the *englyn* to the tradition regarding Llywelyn, who was said to have a hunting lodge here. The greyhound, a present from his father-in-law King John, was famous for hunting. A wolf entered the house when the family was absent; Llywelyn returning was greeted by the dog covered in blood, found the cradle overturned just as in the Jones version and formed the fateful conclusion.

William Alexander Madocks had been left some businesses by his father in the 1790's together with some money in trust for the purchase of land. With this he bought two small farms near Dolgellau, which provided a house, called Dolmelynllyn, where the sociable Madocks started to invite his English friends. He had, by 1800, also bought some land adjoining Traeth Mawr, and set about his ambitious scheme to reclaim the Traeth. He started to improve a house there as well, and he and his friends would come over from

*Plas Tan yr Allt, William Madocks' house
near Traeth Mawr*

Dolgellau to Tan yr Allt to supervise the construction works on the embankment.

Spencer was evidently among the friends from London society whom he invited to Dolgellau and who accompanied him on his trips from there to Tremadoc (on one of which the visit to Beddgelert must have taken place). The Honourable William Robert Spencer was well-known in the clearly clubbish London of Pitt, Fox and Sheridan, and in the literary circles of Scott and Byron, both of whom praised his talent, though he does not seem to have done anything memorable until the publication of his poems in 1811. He is described by at least two reference books as 'poet and wit', an enviable career perhaps and one which may be explained by his family position. He was a Spencer in the Allthorp and Blenheim sense, a grandson of the third Duke of Marlborough, though he died in poverty and obscurity in Paris, in 1834. According to the Encyclopedia Britannica 'among his best-known pieces was the poem 'Beth Gelert'.'

It is a long poem, in lively couplets, 24 stanzas of four lines, rhyming AB throughout, in that ornamentally archaic language which was regarded, during the whole of the 19th century, as the correct language for poetry. It contains a large number of details which are not given in the Edward Jones footnote, though some are hinted at by Bingley, and so once again point to either an independent source or the fictional imagination of the writer. That is: Gelert is Llywelyn's favourite hunting dog, a loyal companion; he was a gift from King John; on the occasion in question he is missing. The hunt that day is not so good, owing to the absence of Gelert. Llywelyn has mixed feelings when Gelert meets him on his return, but in any case sees the blood on the dog's fangs at once and finds the child's bed overturned. (It is interesting that there has been no prior mention of Gelert being left protecting the child in this version). Finding more blood, but no child, he forms the crucial conclusion.

'Hell-hound! My child by thee's devour'd,'
The frantic father cried,
And to the hilt his vengeful sword
He plung'd in Gelert's side.

The dog gives his master a pitiful look; a dying cry from Gelert wakes the child, hidden under a 'mangled heap'. The child is unharmed, but a dead wolf lies by the couch. Llywelyn realizes his mistake:

Ah! what was then Llewelyn's pain!

Bryn y Bedd

For now the truth was clear,
His gallant hound the wolf had slain
To save Llewelyn's heir.

He raises a fine tomb, 'with costly sculpture deck't', which gave
to the place its name, 'Gelert's Grave'.

Of these specific components – the favoured dog, the poor hunt,
the elaborate tomb – none occur in the version given by Borrow,
'known to most people' and a 'popular and most universally
received tradition'. Instead Borrow has Llywelyn encamped in the
valley with a few followers during his military campaign, and the
infant consequently left in its cradle in his tent, Gelert explicitly left
guarding it, after Llywelyn had given the child its fill of goat's milk.
Bingley and Jones both mention a nursery in Llywelyn's house, and
Spencer has the prince returning to his castle. The tent is unique to

Borrow, as is the goat's milk. In Borrow's tale too appears the sentimental detail of the dying dog licking its master's hand.

Jenkins complains that the version given by Sabine Baring-Gould, in *Curious Myths of the Middle Ages* (published 1866), is 'as insipid a version of the Gelert story' as could be given, but he is explicitly comparing it to Spencer's. Jenkins thinks that an essential point missed by Baring-Gould is that Gelert intentionally absented himself from the hunt, having a presentiment of coming danger. It was because Llywelyn was unaware of this that his disappointment with the hunt was tinged with annoyance at Gelert as he rode home. Jenkins says that Llywelyn would not have left Gelert in charge of the baby, as in Baring-Gould, particularly as Gelert was his best hunting dog, because he had servants for the purpose. His critique of the story is in other words curiously literal, but it reveals the extent to which each writer is able to add his own interpretation.

This, then, is perhaps the point, the essential lesson we should draw from comparison of these various original versions, Jones, Bingley, Spencer, Borrow and Baring-Gould. Each telling is enriched by details not present in the others. To conclude, as Jenkins does, that Spencer could not have got it from Jones, 'for Jones did not supply nearly enough for Spencer's purpose' is to argue tendentiously and wrongly. Jenkins wants to say that they both got it from Prichard. But there is no need to infer a common source, since the outline of the tale could by itself have provided the frame on which writers elaborated the theme for their own purposes. Borrow and Spencer would be expected to add their own imaginative details, and in doing so were acting in exactly the manner of traditional story-tellers.

FOUR

BIOGRAPHY OF A LEGEND

The Pancatantra is a treatise on the theory of government in the form of animal-fables, not unlike those of Aesop, composed, probably by a Brahmin (a member of the priestly casts of the Hindu system), sometime before about 550 AD, when it was translated from Sanskrit (the sacred language of India, and that of the educated class) into Pahlavi, the Middle Persian language. Its ultimate origin is unknown, but probably dates to around 300 AD. Each of the animal stories in it contains a moral. Book V is titled 'On Hasty Actions'. Story 1 of that book concerns a Brahmin and his wife.

The wife gave birth to a son, and in accordance with the rites required she went to a stream to wash her clothes and purify herself. The Brahmin was too poor to have servants, and so looked after the child himself. While the wife was away a sacred day in the lunar calendar occurred, and the Brahmin was sent for by the queen to attend a reading of sacred texts. It was an honour which he could not afford to let pass, but there was no-one to look after the child. He therefore left his mongoose guarding the baby, having raised the mongoose in the family home as if it were his own son.

Shortly after the Brahmin had left, the mongoose saw a black cobra, a particularly venomous type of Indian snake, coming out of a hole and approaching the boy – snakes and mongooses being traditional enemies in Indian tales. He pounced on the snake and tore it to pieces. Proud of what he had done he ran to greet the Brahmin on his return, showing his bloody mouth and paws.

> Now, that Brahmin was prone to hasty action, and when he saw the mongoose with his mouth covered with blood, he thought: 'What? He has eaten my son!' and beat the mongoose to death with his stick. After killing him the Brahmin went into his house. Upon entering the house he found his son asleep as he had left him and near by the black cobra torn to pieces.

Nobody who knows the Gelert story could fail to recognize this. The good and loyal creature, it is implied, is unable to speak in its defence. The calumny is acted on hastily. There is then permanent regret for the uncorrectable act once taken.

The Pahlavi edition was translated into Old Syriac about 570 AD and into Arabic about 750. This was an important step in its long life, since under the title 'Kalilah wa Dimnah' it went forward towards its many European translations. It was translated into Greek in the 11th century and thence into Latin between 1263 and 1278. It was also translated abut this time into German and Slavonic. From the Arabic there were Persian and Hebrew translations, but it was the fact that the Latin one was printed in about 1480 that enabled it to spread fast through Europe. An Italian version appeared in 1552 and from that an English translation, by Sir Thomas North, in 1570. It is perhaps from the Latin source, under the title *Historia Septem Sapientum Romae*, 'The Tales of the Seven Sages of Rome', that the material enters Welsh literature, appearing as *Chwedlau Saith Ddoethion Rhufain* amongst the material collected in The Red Book of Hergest. But it is likely that the story's popularity in Europe, after its translation from the Arabic, led to purely folklore versions of it which in due course reached the ears of David Prichard in South Wales or of his immediate informant at Beddgelert. Franklin Edgerton, in his 1924 reconstruction of the Pancatantra, published by the American Oriental Society, has traced the steps by which the story became adapted.

First, the Brahmin became a priest or a monk, in the Arabic version; at the same time the mongoose became a weasel. When an Arab version, the *Sindibad*, became popular in Europe as the *Seven Sages*, a second transformation took place: the priest became a knight, and the weasel became a dog. The snake now becomes anomalous; the wolf is a more natural enemy of the dog, and when the story enters Wales that last transformation takes place. The faithful dog is of course a type in Welsh story, as for instance Arthur's dog Cafall, mentioned in the tale of Culhwch and Olwen.

Sabine Baring-Gould (mentioned in the last chapter as being criticized by Jenkins) traced a number of different animals in the story in its widespread forms. It is, he says, a pole-cat in the Mongolian translation of the Tibetan Dsanglun, a cat in the Persian Sindibad-nameh, and has become a dog before the Hebrew translation. Baring-Gould also relates the story to a body of lore concerned with grateful animals attempting to do humans favours and being misunderstood. There is, apparently, a saint in France whose origins were as a dog. St Guinefort, though never recognized as a saint by the church, has been the subject of a local cult near Lyon since the 13th century. The story is the same as the Gelert one – a knight went hunting, leaving his child in the care of the dog; he came back to find the dog bloody, the room disturbed; he formed the wrong conclusion and killed the dog. Then the child cried, and he found it safe and the dead body of its intending attacker, still here a snake. A shrine arose for Guinefort, the dog, and in due course miracles occurred and the dog became venerated as a saint.

44

Joseph Jacobs, referred to above, remarks after tracing the story's literary route 'from India to Wales': 'We have still to connect the legend with Llewelyn and with Bedd Gelert'. He says first of all that it is not impossible that it should be true. 'The saving of an infant's life by a dog, and the mistaken slaughter of the dog, are not such an improbable combination as to make it impossible that the same event occurred in many places.' He regards it as impossible, however, that the event should have been used in the same way in so any places as a warning against rash action. He finds examples of the imagery in local place-names and artifacts – it occurs, for instance, in a stone sculpture in Co. Limerick and a tombstone in Abergavenny – and sees it as embodied in the Welsh national crest (of a greyhound) adopted in the time of Richard III.

The final step to localizing it at Beddgelert he identifies as that referred to in the last chapter, the presence there of a local legend about a dog named Cylart, which was recorded in Edward Jones's *Musical Relics*, in 1784, and so, we may safely say, present in the town before David Prichard ever came there.

Five

WELCOME TO FAIRYLAND

Perhaps some explanation of how a town could come to be known through a fictional story lies in a realization of the sort of place it is. We remarked in a previous chapter that Beddgelert evidently bears an innate fertility for matters of the imagination, and this is well borne-out by a further look. At one side of it lies the site of a fundamental basis of Welsh mythology: Dinas Emrys, the place of origin of both the wizard Merlin and the imagery of the red dragon.

Dinas Emrys

At the other side lies the home of the fairies.

The area of Beddgelert parish known as Nant Colwyn lies between the village and Rhyd-ddu, and more specificaly a stretch of this on the Drws y Coed side, lying between Cwm Hafod Ruffydd and Llyn y Dwarchen is known as *Gwlad y Tylwyth Teg*, the land of the fairies. The heartland of this might be regarded as Pont Cae'r Gors, where the winding road crosses the Colwyn stream and the woods touch the bottom of the valley.

It is perhaps necessary at this point to dispel some illusions. These fairies do not fly, let alone adopt such miniature forms as would have them flitting from flower to flower. Such pretty Victorian fancies are alien to them. These are fairies of a more robust and ancient kind.

They are in general small but not of non-human form. You might mistake them at a distance for a crowd of children. They are

Cwm Hafod Ruffydd lies at one side of
Gwlad y Tylwyth Teg, *the land of the fairies*

Pont Cae'r Gors

otherwise like rather delicate human beings. The types vary, however, from region to region, and as analysed by Sir John Rhys, in *Celtic Folklore*, and by David Jenkins in his *Bedd Gelert*, they come in two main types.

> In some places the *Tylwyth Teg* are described as a small folk of a thieving nature, living in summer among the fern bushes in the mountains, and in winter in the heather and gorse ... In other districts the fairies were described as a little bigger and stronger folk; but these latter were also of a thieving disposition.

So Rhys wrote, in the 1880's. And Jenkins confirms this, unsurprisingly since he is translating from the same source, William Jones's articles in *Y Brython*, and since he reveals he has already read Rhys.

Nant Colwyn above Pont Cae'r Gors

Fairies were not all of the same species, but were almost invariably associated with hilly districts. They varied according to the districts to which they belonged just as human beings differ according to the difference of the surroundings amid which the have been reared. In some districts the fairies are described as diminutive beings with strong thieving propensities, who used to live in summer among the bracken on the mountains and in winter among the heather and gorse.

Both authorities then assert that there is yet a third kind. Rhys says

There is still another species of *Tylwyth Teg*, very unlike the foregoing ones in their nature and habits. Not only was this last kind far more beautiful and comely than the others, but they were honest and good towards mortals. Their whole nature was replete with joy and fun, nor were they ever beheld hardly except engaged in some merry-making or other. They might be seen on bright moonlight nights at it, singing and carolling playfully on the fair meadows and the green slopes ... Though it used to be said that they were spiritual and immortal beings, still they ate and drank like human beings: they married and had children.

Jenkins again paraphrases this passage. Rhys locates the areas where this third type may be found – they favour 'rushy combes surrounded by smooth hills with round tops, also the banks of river and the borders of lakes; but they were seldom seen at any time near rocks or cliffs'. Penmachno, Dolwyddelan, the sides of Moel Siabod, Llandegai Mountains ... and 'the upper portion of the parish of Beddgelert from Drwys y Coed to the Pennant ...' These beings lived underground, and emerged through overhanging banks of pools or lakes; they came out sometimes in broad daylight, 'two or three together, and now and then a shepherd, so the saying went, used to talk and chat with them.' But their true time was the full moon, when they held a party. They sang and danced from midnight to cock-crow, and many people went to watch them, though it was dangerous to go too near: if you intruded into their circle they cast a spell over you and you disappeared. It was possible to rescue someone who had been so trapped, but only if done before cock-crow and the disappearance of the whole crowd. You need a long stick of mountain ash, because the fairies cannot touch that; you obtrude the end of it into the dancing circle, and when the mortal comes round in the dance he can grab hold of it and you can pull him out.

Rhys says that his information comes from Mr. William Jones of Llangollen, who was 'the best living authority I have found on the folklore of Beddgelert, Drws y Coed, and the surrounding district'. Jones mentions some first-hand accounts, in his articles in *Y Brython*, which Rhys translates:

> In the north-west corner of the parish of Beddgelert there is a place which used to be called by the old inhabitants the Land of the Fairies, and it reached from Cwm Hafod Ruffydd along the slopes of the mountain of Drws y Coed as far as Llyn y Dywarchen. The old people of former times used to find much pleasure and amusement in this district in listening every moonlight night to the charming music of the fair family, and in looking at their dancing and their mirthful sports.

It might be noted that Rhys here translates *Y Tylwyth Teg* as 'the fair family', and personally I do not think the translation 'fairies' does them justice, since Tylwyth Teg means something more specific. Though the 'teg' bit is indirectly connected with 'fair' as in 'fairy', *tylwyth* means family in the sense of ancestry and so would relate the beings to a belief in ancestral spirits. It is clear that they live in a world like ours but without the dimension of time: those who have been entrapped by them may return after years thinking only a few minutes have passed. To that extent they do not live in Nant Colwyn but in Annwn, the old Celtic otherworld, the Welsh equivalent of the Irish realm of Tir-na-nOg. There the people of the mythological time survive unaged, the race which inhabited this land in a time before we came, the people of the Goddess Danaan, the Sidhe, the followers of Gwyn ap Nudd, *Yr Hen Bobl*, the people who were here before us.

This, at any rate, is the thinking arrived at by John Owen Huws, in his invaluable book *Y Tylwyth Teg*. He traces the Welsh belief in a counterpart people back to the Mabinogion, where they occur in the story of Lludd and Llefelys as 'the Corianiaid'. These occurred as a plague in the kingdom ruled by Lludd, and were invincible because they could hear everything that was said. Lludd is advised by his brother Llefelys to prepare some special water with which to sprinkle the people, both his own folk and those of the alien race. The latter would be destroyed by it. We are reminded of the means by which St Collen destroyed the illusion created by the fairyfolk, the followers of Gwyn ap Nudd, on top of Glastonbury Tor. The saint, though sceptical, had taken to the meeting some holy water, and when he doused the assembled company of otherworldly beings with it they disappeared.

There is no doubt from the accounts by Rhys, Jenkins and Huws that the folklorists they report had believed that such counterpart people had been not just a symbolic presence but a reality, in the sense of being observable by experience at least at a time in the past. Jenkins believes this, following William Jones, and Rhys comes to the same conclusion from his various informants, then in their old age. As a noted academic, holder of the chair of Celtic at Oxford, Rhys feels obliged to excuse his time spent studying

Llyn y Gadair, Rhyd-ddu and Snowdon

folklore, but he believes that 'As a reality to those who believed in them, the superstitions of our ancestors form an integral part of their history ... [and] it is a mark of an uncultured people not to know or care to know the history of the race'. But Huws goes further. He is not reporting something heard from an old man about his grandparents in the second half of the 19th century. He carried out his firsthand research in Snowdonia in the 1970's, and published his book in 1987. He says in the Introduction that he has known three men, now in their maturity; who saw the Tylwyth Teg. The dramatist Wil Sam saw one when having a sly smoke as a child. According to his description the one he saw gave him a nasty look. The late W. J. Jones, from Dyffryn Nantlle (near Rhyd-ddu) saw one of the Tylwyth Teg dancing, when he was a child, and he had the witness of his brother who was with him at the time. A third person,

Owen Ellis Pritchard, also saw one dancing on a rock, on land on the slopes of Tryfan.

These are explicit claims to have had experiences in the normal world of something which is not regarded as normal. Current belief on the matter tends to be more equivocal, as when Sir T. H. Parry-Williams, Professor of Welsh at the University of Wales, Aberystwyth, himself originally from Rhyd-ddu, was asked directly on a radio programme if he believed in the Tylwyth Teg. He answered, 'No,' but then added: 'but they do exist'.

Some years ago when involved in a television programme to mark the centenary of the opening of the Snowdon railway I was told in all seriousness that one problem it had given rise to was the effect on the Tylwyth Teg. The fairy people of the southern slopes of Snowdon became confined, and started to become more troublesome in the valleys to the south, because they could not cross the line of continuous metal. Presumably the reopening of the Welsh Highland Railway through Rhyd-ddu to Beddgelert will give rise to a similar problem.

There is no doubt that these reporters and their informants wish their descriptions to be taken literally, in the sense that they saw something in the normal way of seeing: and if we on our part wish to claim that they did not experience creatures from another world, or another dimension of this one, on the grounds that there is no such thing, we should have to say firstly how we could be so sure, and secondly what it was that they saw.

The second plague which befell the kingdom of Lludd (in the story, the founder of London, and so the equivalent of King Lud) also concerns us here, in this magical and secluded area to the south of Snowdon. The story in the Mabinogion tells how the hill of Dinas Emrys became the repository of a mystical burial, the uncovering of which gave rise to a reawakening of Welsh identity.

The remains of a medieval castle can be seen near the summit of Dinas Emrys

The cause of the plague is two fighting dragons – the native dragon and 'a dragon of another foreign people'. Lludd is to entice them into a sheet placed in a pit, and when they fall asleep there to bury them in the most secure place in the kingdom. As long as they are in that secure place, no plague will come to Britain from elsewhere. Lludd found that the safest place in his kingdom was Dinas Emrys, and he buried them there.

That would have been the outcome of the story had it not been for a later period of disruption. King Vortigern was obliged to confront the Saxons, who had come to the island by his invitation but were threatening to dominate it. At a meeting at Stonehenge he was betrayed by them, and his people were slaughtered. He himself escaped and was advised to retreat to the safest place in his kingdom. He came to Dinas Emrys.

Though he tried to build a castle there, it seemed the place was

The marshy hollow on the hilltop of Dinas Emrys shows where a pool had been cut in the Roman period

bewitched: as much as he built during the day disappeared at night. He consulted his wise men, and was told that he had to sacrifice on the spot a boy who had no father. Messengers were sent out, and a boy who claimed to have no father found, in the town of Carmarthen. On the hilltop he demanded the right to ask a question of the wise men. What was buried in the marshy hollow below the summit of Dinas Emrys? We know, of course, having read the Mabinogion. The wise men were ignorant, but duly dug up the dragons.

The boy was Emrys, or Ambrose, in history the Roman-Briton Ambrosius, a prototype of King Arthur who led the resistance of the post-Roman Britons to the Saxons invasion. In the expansion of the story in Geoffrey of Monmouth's *The History of the Kings of Britain* he becomes Merlin, and it is on this hilltop that he first proclaims his prophecies. Following the original story in Nennius, Geoffrey says that the boy-prophet said that the dragons would fight, the white one (the dragon of a foreign people) appearing to defeat the red, the native dragon. But the red dragon would revive and win in the end.

Excavations carried out in the 1950's revealed that the hilltop of Dinas Emrys has indeed long been fortified: the square base of a medieval castle is still visible, but the hill was occupied as early as the Roman period. Of course its precipitous sides and its views both ways along the pass make it highly defensible. It was a notable 'Dark Age' site, with pieces of amphorae and ornaments indicating a fairly sophisticated court towards the end of the fifth century. The amazing thing is the apparent confirmation of the myth. There was indeed (the excavators found) a covered pool on the summit plateau, in a deep hollow which you can see today in the form of a patch of reeds. The pool was found to be man-made, a sort of cistern, probably cut during the early-Roman period and so in the time of Lludd rather than Ambrosius.

So we confront here not just an unscathed Welsh terrain but a flashback in the history of human imagination, in a world of scrub oak and bracken, where the moss climbs to the tops of the trees, and only the sounds of birds emphasise a silence which hangs about this untouched place, unmarked for the last few thousand years.

SIX

THE REAL CELERT

'… seated in a beautiful tract of meadows, at the junction of three vales, near the conflux of the *Glas Lyn* and the *Colwyn*, which flows through Nant Colwyn, a vale that leads to *Caernarvon*. Its situation was the fittest in the world to inspire religious meditation, amidst lofty mountains, wood, and murmuring streams.' Pennant perhaps connects the three-pronged junction with ideas of trinity; now we might not immediately identify as religion the state most fostered by Beddgelert, rather than, say, imagination. Yet it does seem as if religion was the form which its inspiration took from an early period.

There is, to begin with, the possibility that Christianity had already taken root in the 'Dark Age' settlement on Dinas Emrys. One of the more notable finds of the 1950's excavation was a small piece of pottery which may perhaps have formed part of the base of a plate. It contains quite clearly the marks of a stamped decoration which includes the 'Chi-Rho' emblem, the symbols for the first two letters of the word Christ in the Greek alphabet, within the framework of a cross. Such positively Christian symbolism is rare, in probably the sixth century, and of course we do not know where the small clay item came from before it got lost at Dinas Emrys. We do know that Christianity arrived and grew in the valley in early monastic times.

Giraldus Cambrensis, who travelled through this area while on

Conflux of Glaslyn and Colwyn

his journey with Archbishop Baldwin to raise support for the third crusade, does not mention Beddgelert in his Itinerary or his Description of Wales, but he clearly refers to it, though not by name, in his other book, the 'Mirror of the Church'. It was then, quite clearly, the seat of a major religious house, of the order of the Culdees, a particularly intensive eremitic religious group which later largely became absorbed into the Augustinians:

> There was in Gwynedd, which is popularly known as North Wales, a religious house of clerics under the foot of the mountain of Eryri which is commonly called Snowdon, that is Mountain of Snow, not far from the place known as the court of Merlin Ambrosius [i.e. Dinas Emrys], fairly close to the shore of the Irish sea.

St Mary's Church, Beddgelert, from the west

These clerics were at this time, he says, bound to no particular order, but were celibates and *colidei*, that is worshippers of god, noted for abstinence, good works, and hospitality. It was undoubtedly this early monastic group that developed into the major monastery of St Mary which was recognized in the next century as (though still small in numbers) important in the structure of Welsh religion.

We know of it first during a time of conflict and in the aftermath of a disaster. It is often assumed that the army of Edward I was in this area during his last war with Llywelyn. For instance, Black's Guide of 1891 (drawing on Pennant) states, of the valley of Nantlle: 'In this vicinity Edward I. encamped his army when engaged in subjugating the principality.' It adds that he spent the summer of 1284 in a farm-house near the lakes. It is possible (whether or not this is true) that the policy of forest-clearance, either to remove cover or to enable movement of troops, which may have been employed at this time on the route of the Roman road to Caernarfon, was responsible for the fire which destroyed the Abbey of St Mary at Beddgelert in 1286. Certainly (as Alan Bott and Margaret Dunn point out in their history of the Priory and Church) Llywelyn accused the English of burning churches; and in a famous letter from Bishop Anian of Bangor seeking funds for rebuilding the monastery it was said to have been 'totally destroyed by an accidental fire'. Because that fire destroyed the monastery's records it is that letter that forms Beddgelert's entry into history:

> Whereupon, know all, that the said house of the Blessed Mary is the senior religious house in all Wales (except the Island of Saints, Bardigeya), and of better hospitality and of more common resort for the poor, and for the English and Welsh travellers, for those passing from England and West Wales to North Wales, and for those going from Ireland and North Wales into England.

Thus it is the Priory which is referred to first, as being a hospitable posting point for travellers, and evidence of the place itself which grew up around it to begin with exists only in passing references. A charter of the last Llywelyn, of 1258, is witnessed by the Prior of 'Bekelert', and the name takes the form 'Bedkelerd' in a document of 1269. Edward himself gave a charter to 'Brother Madoc, Prior of the House of the Blessed Mary of Bethkelert ...' where all previous charters and 'all the buildings of the Priory itself' have been unfortunately lately burnt.

There is, then, no certainty that the name originated with the distinctive, and unusual, spelling *bedd*. The matter is debated closely, because to some early antiquarians it seemed possible that

61

it was derived from bwth, a hut, and so to refer to a cell of an early hermit. Jenkins however has a firm opinion on the subject. It is, according to him, the site of a grave.

The name, he points out, long precedes the introduction of the dog story. He points out that the old cowshed (which he dates as late eighteenth century) near the 'Grave' stands on a green hillock, which 'from time immemorial ... has been called "Bryn y Bedd", a name which most people would now explain as being due to its proximity to the dog's grave.' There are, he says, other views about the cowshed, some saying it was built from the ruins of Llywelyn's summer residence, others that it was made of the ruins of the Prior's palace. The green hill, Bryn y Bedd, was more conspicuous before it was levelled 'to facilitate the erection of this plain structure'.

At a time when John Prichard had succeeded his father David as landlord of the Goat a large tree was removed from the western

The hill known as Bryn y Bedd was levelled to construct the cowshed

side of this hillock. Prichard, like his father, was interested in local history, and he had the mound investigated, hoping to find the foundations of an old building. All they found were stones, which, Jenkins says, 'must have once been in the bed of a river': in other words they were rounded, probably glacial deposits. 'So Mr. Prichard felt quite satisfied that there had been no building of any kind on the spot.'

But what, Jenkins asks, does such a heap of rounded stones imply? Ignoring the glacial explanation, he concludes they must have been brought there intentionally. The only purpose, he reasons, 'must have been to form a cairn or a mound of mixed earth and stones.' It was a grave. Whose grave?

Sir John Rhys informed Joseph Jacobs (author of *Celtic Fairy Tales*) that the form rt in the name Celert makes it 'un-Welsh'. Jenkins points to a list of Irish chieftains who apparently came into this part of Wales in the fourth century, among whom is Celert, son of Math, son of Mathonwy. But he gains his information from a work in the collection of Iolo Morganwg, at the time still a revered source for Welsh antiquarianism, later revealed as a forger and inventor. (Jenkins shows that doubts were already growing regarding Iolo's work, when he says 'We cannot vouch for the correctness of this list …') His solution to the 'name-problem', that 'Bryn y Bedd is the burial mound of the Irish chief Celert, and the village is called after him 'Bedd Gelert', is therefore in doubt as soon as he has raised it.

The most likely explanation in the end is the most obvious. Somewhere here is the grave of the founding 'saint'. His name was not Celert, but Celer, and we know this because he is better known elsewhere.

Llangeler is a small compact town on the A484 east of Newcastle Emlyn in Carmarthenshire. The church there which is

St Celer's church at Llangeler,
in south-western Wales

dedicated to St Celer is a sturdy grey structure occupying a clearly older religious site. It is said to be the successor of a chapel dedicated to St Mary (like the Priory at Beddgelert) itself located at the site of a holy well, an instance of which is also mentioned by Jenkins as having at one time existed at Beddgelert but been neglected and filled in. The churchyard at Llangeler is circular, which is said to be the sign of a very old settlement.

There is a chapel dedicated to St Celer also at Llandysul, some three miles east of Llangeler, indicating that perhaps he was more involved in this area than further north; but it must be said that nothing is known of him, and the speculation that he was a Dark Age hermit is based on probability, by inference from other known instances of early church associations. Among much else that is not known about him is why he came to be buried in northern Wales on the road to Caernarfon.

The church which survives there now contains some physical evidence of the great Priory of which it once formed a part, 13th century work forming the chancel and perhaps some even older work being indicated around the west door. Bott and Dunn (in their history of the Priory and the church) give the opinion that a major sponsor might be seen to be involved, and since the work dates from between 1220 and 1240 the evidence would point to Llywelyn the Great, whose positive interest in monastic works throughout what was then Gwynedd is well established. Although Jenkins attributes the church's original endowment to Owain Gwynedd (d.1170) this is not the date of the main period of building as evidenced by its remains today. Anian's letter, and Edward I's charter which follows it, both cite Llywelyn as the first to grant this Priory official recognition.

Nothing else of the Priory can be seen now above ground, but in Jenkins's time there still remained a memory of it having been visible, 'an extensive old ruin on the southern side of the church' which the old people called Plas Prior, evidently thought to be the Prior's palace. 'The foundations of these still exist in some places', he says. Work on the churchyard in the mid 19th century had revealed the bases of walls, and grave-digging had turned up coins of the reign of Henry III. Jenkins is consistent with modern thinking

The stone base of Llywelyn's coffin – originally at Aberconwy Abbey, then moved to Maenan Abbey and eventually housed at Gwydir Chapel in the church at Llanrwst afer the Dissolution

in identifying the present church as that of the abbey, become the parish church on the Dissolution, as happened in Conwy when the monastery was moved.

Pennant speaks of the church as being small but 'the loftiest in Snowdonia', and Jenkins leaves us in no doubt that before the 19th century restorations it was something of a magnificent specimen, a feast of carved wood and coloured glass with a steep-shelved roof and an air of ancientness increased by encroaching trees and a mass of ivy on the gables. Jenkins has nothing but bitterness to express about the 1830 changes: '… one thing is certain, and that is that it is very difficult to speak of their work except as a piece of vicious Vandalism'. The church was made to look from the outside like a

Nant Gwynant

barn, 'one of the primitive Nonconformist meeting houses', with a low roof and plain windows. The famed woodwork was sold to the people of the parish, who used it for firewood and furniture, and the windows sold to an English firm. Now, after an extensive exercise in repointing of the outside and redesigning of the interior decoration, with the result that the church today presents a pleasant a cared-for appearance, its condition, claim Bott and Dunn, is 'better than at any time since at least the Reformation'.

Great events of the outside world have swept past Beddgelert and left their mark, as Edward I's conquest did in his restoration of the Priory and Henry VIII's break with Rome in the effects of the Dissolution of the Monasteries. The various turmoils to which Wales has been subjected in between have penetrated even these

The popular path along the river bank towards 'Gelert's Grave'

mountain valleys, borne no doubt by the pull of the old road to Segontium. The Prior of Beddgelert was, for instance, one of the supporters of Owain Glyndŵr, and in due course became outlawed for that commitment by the victorious king. It is said that in the meantime Glyndŵr himself had spent part of his outlawed time hiding in a cave not far away, on Moel yr Ogof, between Beddgelert and the Pennant valley.

Beddgelert however did not come back into the forefront of public interest until the early 19th century, when, in 1805, a new turnpike road came up through Aberglaslyn to link by way of Nant Gwynant to Lord Penrhyn's road at Capel Curig. It was about this time that another royal prince came, the event adding the 'royal' to the name of the Goat Hotel.

The visit of Prince Arthur, Duke of Connaught, is recounted by

Jenkins as something of a comedy. A reception party consisting of the whole population was assembled to greet his expected arrival. But instead of driving in style into the village he dismissed his carriage at the Aberglaslyn Pass and walked up the river. He appeared, incognito, with a couple of friends, walking across the field past Gelert's Grave.

In Jenkins's time the village had not forgotten another famous visitor, the writer Charles Kingsley, who had become famous as the author of *Westward Ho!*. Kingsley's book *Two Years Ago*, published in 1857, is actually set in the West Country, but a sequence of it takes place based at Beddgelert which includes a description of the Penygwryd Hotel and some dramatic mountaineering passages.

Among the memorabilia displayed on the walls of the Tanronnen Hotel today, perhaps one of the most puzzling is a photograph of a young-looking Paul McCartney posing with a middle-aged man on a cottage doorstep. It is an image which expresses in the present world Beddgelert's lasting ability to influence imagination.

In 1994 the Followers of Rupert instigated a picnic site at a spot called Cae Gel, on the other side of the Glaslyn river from the church. It was to commemorate the fact that the graphic artist Alfred

The Tanronnen Hotel sign in the centre of Beddgelert

*Paul McCartney and his young family with Alfred Bestall, the graphic designer of
'Rupert the Bear' at his home in Beddgelert
(Photo: Tanronnen Hotel, Beddgelert)*

Bestall had lived for much of the time until he died in 1986 in a
nearby cottage, Penlan, which he had bought in 1956. McCartney
had visited him there in the 1970's.

Of the several artists who have been responsible for establishing
the image of Rupert Bear, Bestall was regarded as the most
definitive, and he was solely responsible for drawing and writing

the Express's Rupert cartoon from 1935 until the 1960's and continued the produce the text for the annual into the 1970's. Consequently it is hardly surprising that he was known as 'Mr. Rupert Bear' in the village which he had made his permanent home for the last years of his life. Bestell (who initially lived in Surbiton, and was an illustrator for Punch) had first come to north Wales as a child, and had formed the habit of visiting several times a year.

It is said that, at least during his time as Rupert's creator, the surroundings of Nutwood developed a ruggedness about them and a wooded complexity which showed the influence of Bestall's home landscape at Beddgelert. Such matters however will have to be left to better qualified authorities to determine.

It seems quite likely though that Bestall would have recognized Beddgelert and its surroundings as a world in which your fantasies can flourish.

Acknowledgements

The author wishes to thank Margaret Dunn and Richard Neale for their help in supplying information.

Bibliography

Baring-Gould, Sabine: *Myths of the Middle Age*, Ed. John Matthews, Blandford, London 1996.

Bingley, Rev. W.: *North Wales*, Denbighshire County Council.

Borrow, George: *Wild Wales*, Oxford University Press, 1946.

Bott, Alan; Dunn, Margaret: *A Guide to the Priory and Parish Church of St Mary, Beddgelert.*

Daniels, Ann; Neale, Richard: *Beddgelert and Nantgwynant – Walks*, National Trust.

Giraldus Cambrensis: *The Itinerary through Wales*, Everyman, 1935.

Gwyndaf, Robin: *Welsh Folk Tales*, National Museums and Galleries of Wales, Cardiff, 1999.

Huws, John Owen: *Y Tylwyth Teg*, Gwasg Carreg Gwalch, Llanrwst, 1987.

Jacobs, Joseph: *Celtic Fairy Tales*, Bodley Head, London, 1970 (First published 1891).

Jenkins, D. E.: *Bedd Gelert – Its Fact, Fairies and Folklore*, Portmadoc, 1899. Facsimile edition 1999, Friends of St Mary's Church, Beddgelert.

Kingsley, Charles: *Two Years Ago*, Macmillan, London, 1895.

Pennant, Thomas: *Tours in Wales*, Caernarvon, 1883.

Rhys, John: *Celtic Folklore*, Oxford, 1901. Wildwood, London, 1980.

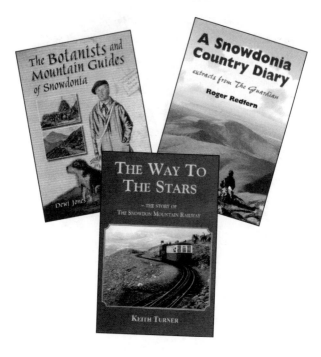

Also of interest ....

Visit our website for further information:
www.carreg-gwalch.com

Orders can be placed on our
On-line Shop

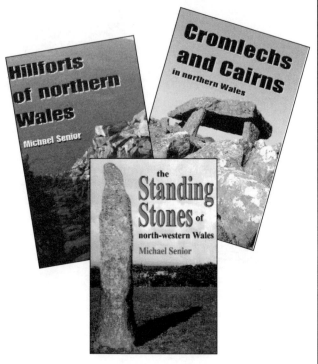